THE CRITICAL PATH

Kant's Transcendental Idealism

Barry John Hanton

"The critical path alone is still open"

Immanuel Kant

For Reverend

John Charles Whitney

a shepherd of Christ

PREFACE

In what follows I have tried to present the thought of Immanuel Kant in as simple language as possible. I have tried to elucidate the thinking of all three of his *Critiques*, that of pure reason, practical reason, and of aesthetic judgement. This decision is based on my contention that these two latter works contain the fullness of what Kant actually set out to achieve in writing the first. Without this rounded out understanding of his critical system, it is all too easy to misunderstand Kant's philosophy, the result being the widespread misrepresentation of him as a merely technical thinker who does nothing to address man's existential concerns.

I hope somebody finds it to be of value.

INTRODUCTION

The philosopher and mathematician A.N. Whitehead once said that all philosophy was mere footnotes to Plato. Similarly, it could be stated fairly, and without exaggeration that all philosophy subsequent to the life-work of Immanuel Kant (1724-1804) is of the same relative status. The entire philosophical *opus* of Kant is often mistakenly envisaged as being equivalent to his first *Critique*, that of pure reason. And although this mighty tome was of profound and lasting influence, his ideas ranged far beyond the confines of that first critique, not only in breadth of content, but in depth. In the works consequential to the *Critique of Pure Reason* (1781), Kant's thinking penetrated into depths of being to a measure that could reasonably argued to be unequalled. On the far side of what can be seen, due to Kant's tight, dense writing style, as the technical formality of the first critique lies the metaphysical deeps of the *Critique of Practical Reason* (1788). For Kant was not the superficial, proto-positivist that he would come to be seen as by some Anglo-American philosophers of the 20th century, indeed, his thinking shares very little common ground with the stultifying aridity of so-called analytic philosophy. Whilst Kant's musings began with the laying out of the ground within which any fruitful thinking could come to presence, it did not end there. After the initial, and necessary, ground clearing, his thought moves into the matters of free will, immortality, the human soul, and God Almighty. That is to say, Kant thinks the final things. And whilst Kant is not the most difficult philosopher to understand, he is the most easily *misunderstood*.

To understand Kant, just as any other thinker, we have to grasp his thinking as something that arose as a response to the philosophical conundrums of his own time. Kant thought a middle path between two philosophical extremes, one of them was idealism, the belief that all knowledge is ultimately consciousness knowing itself in one way or another; the other being empiricism, a position that holds all possible knowledge to be experience based. Kant walked a middle path between these two, seeing knowledge as experience based but essentially ordered by consciousness.

Kant's first critique is often framed within the context of the question of what we can know, and this is largely true, but all thought of epistemology is also metaphysics, must be necessarily, how can we ask after knowing what we do not thereby affirm the existence of? Another common misconception about Kant's thought is that it delimited what could be usefully thought. Again, this is true in a sense, but equally misleading. Kant explored the limits of what we could rightfully claim to have a certain kind of knowledge of, by which he meant discreet, scientific knowledge. Kant's philosophical project was not a forerunner of that of the logical positivists of the early 20th century, who sought to *rule out* the possibility of thinking philosophically about anything outside of the subjects they personally considered to be worthy. On the contrary, Kant found that the most significant matters of human life were precisely those things that lay beyond the scope of a certain kind of knowledge. Kant's message was that it is a great mistake for us to try to enframe (to borrow a term from the later Heidegger) all things within such lifeless, technical confines. Thinking about the beauty and depth of being can be fortuitous, but we must never confuse this thinking with what the sciences can teach. This prepares the way for the second *Critique*, that of practical reason. It is in this work that Kant begins to develop his thought regarding the ultimate questions.

In his introduction to the first *Critique* Kant tells us that we can be certain, that there can be no doubt, that our knowledge begins with experience. Our knowledge begins with experience because this is how we come into contact with the world which is the object of all of our knowing. Contrary to the empiricists, however, he rejects the idea that human consciousness is a blank slate onto which the world imprints itself through the senses, as though our thoughts were a kind of inner model, a reconstruction in consciousness of the outside world. We can think of the empiricist position as envisioning the mind as a dark room, and the five senses as apertures into which the outside world pours like sunlight through a window. The resulting light of the room is what we call knowledge. If we may take the liberty of framing these philosophies in the form of caricatures, bearing in mind that no philosopher would ever be this naïve, we could say that the empiricist believes we know only our senses, whilst the idealist believes that we know only our thoughts.

Picture a human being who from birth had been confined inside a sensory depravation tank, a terrible thought I know, but philosophy is a demanding mistress! What would this poor soul know? We answer "nothing at all", which the empiricist receives as the confirmation of his conviction. But Kant discovered a problem which he believed the empiricist machine could not process: he called this the synthetic *a priori*.

Some things can be known to us to be true or false by necessity, logical propositions, for example. The truth of the following syllogism: All dogs are animals, my pet is a dog, therefore my pet is an animal; this is an example of something true by definition. We do not have to make efforts to find out the truth or falsity of a logical statement, we can determine its truth or falsehood before any possible experience. Perhaps I do not even have any pets, the syllogism above still holds. These things are truths *a priori*, true prior to any experiential confirmation. Contrasted with these are propositions which we discover the truth value of only by virtue of experience. I say that it is 3 o'clock and I only know if this is true or false by looking at the clock. I ascertain whether it is true or false after the experience of checking, it is discovered to be true or false *a posteriori*. All well and good. Kant's name for all statements whose truth can only be established *a posteriori* "synthetic judgements". Whereas those which can be judged *a priori* he calls "analytic", for all we need do is to analyse the terms of the statement in order to make a judgement. As long as these two categories remain distinct from each other, Kant thought, then empiricism does well in its explanatory efforts. However, what would happen if we could give an example of an *a priori* truth which could also be found to be true synthetically, through experience? A primary example Kant uses of the synthetic *a priori* is Euclid's definition of the shortest distance between two points being a straight line. This is a statement we know to be true without going out into the world and measuring between any two arbitrary points. However, were we to make such measurements we would *also* find it to be true by experience. It is a synthetic *a priori* truth.

It is obvious why the existence of such statements is so problematic to empiricism. Put in the form of a syllogism, Kant is saying: if empiricism holds then all knowledge of the outside world is ascertained through experience, given the presence of a synthetic *a priori* truth there is knowledge of the world that can be learned prior to experience, therefore empiricism does not hold. Kant believed he had disclosed a difficulty which is insurmountable for empiricism, but it was far from an end in itself, because if this is indeed the case, that there are synthetic *a priori* truths, then which philosophical position could possibly account for them? The answer is what Kant called his own philosophical work that unfolded from his investigation into this question: "Transcendental Idealism".

1: TRANSCENDENTAL AESTHETIC

The names Kant chose for the different regions of his thought are terrifying at first acquaintance: the metaphysical deduction, the transcendental unity of apperception, etc. We begin with the transcendental aesthetic.

Firstly, we must avoid getting off on the wrong foot. We are most familiar with the term "aesthetic" in reference to judgements of the relative beauty of appearances, and in a much later part of his thinking Kant will use the term in this way. A thing is aesthetically pleasing to us if we consider it to look good. Kant does not mean anything like that, and what he subsequently says will be incomprehensible if we do not dismiss this immediately. Aesthetic, in the transcendental aesthetic, refers to the appearance of things to our senses, how things show themselves to be, the way they are given over to us. Appearance is the appearance of a phenomenon. Beyond this we must lay down the foundation of more terminology.

The manner or means by which human knowledge relates to the objects of its knowledge is called intuition. Intuition is the point of connection between us and the objects of the world of our experience. Intuition is always *given* to us, we are the receivers of intuitions. Kant seems to use the term to refer to the immediacy of interactions with the world, perhaps something akin to what we experience in what contemporary philosophers call phenomenal consciousness.

That which makes possible, that allows us to be the kind of beings who can be given intuitions, is something Kant calls our sensibility. Sensibility is the horizon of intuitive reception.

Whilst sensibility is the ground of the reception of intuition, "understanding" is the name Kant gives to the faculty that deals with them, the understanding *thinks* the intuitions. And this thinking of intuitions by the understanding, by virtue of sensibility, is the furnace from which our conceptions are forged. It is important to state explicitly that Kant is not claiming that we receive the intuitions through sensibility and then our thinking generates conceptions as though it were a machine-like function, he is talking about the spontaneous, in real terms inseparable, processes of perception and thought.

All of our thinking about objects must ultimately be related to the reception of intuitions and our ability to receive them, sensibility, because this is how we make contact with objects.

The manner or mode by which our sensibility is

affected by objects is called sensation. Sensation is the primal matter of sensibility; sensibility receives sensation as a plant receives light. This reception Kant calls empirical intuition, it relates us to an object via sensation. The object of an empirical intuition is called a phenomenon, from the Greek *phainesthai*, to appear.

When we receive a sensation, Kant calls that which corresponds to the sensation the *matter* of the phenomenon, its *whatness*. What we feel is the essence, or identity of the phenomenon he calls its form. Kant says that we could not derive the form of the object from any sensation, and this turns out to be radically consequential as Kant will ascribe the form of the phenomenon to our consciousness, and the matter to the object.

If we think of an object, let it be the box I see before me. It is wooden, brown, varnished but uncoloured, it displays the brand of the whiskey glasses it contains. Were I to touch it I would find it to be hard, quite smooth, of room temperature. Now let us imagine that we could remove these properties from the box. We can imagine the box as no longer smooth, no longer room temperature, no longer bearing a brand name. Kant says that we could imagine removing all but two aspects of the box, its spatiality and its presence in time, these two things could not be imagined as ever being removed from the object, and Kant concludes from this impossibility of removing these aspects, that we could not ever have been given them in our sensibility. If this is truly the case, that we could not *learn* of space and time through sensibility, where do they come from? Kant's original and remarkable answer to this question is that they must be part of the inherent structure of consciousness.

Space, as an internal feature of consciousness, is how we represent *to ourselves* the externality of the world, it is a pre-condition of the possibility of experience. We can know objects in the world only because our consciousness is so constituted that it is the basis on which objects are given over to us as experienceable things. And just as we have this external intuition that is called space, so too do we have an internal intuition by which we understand ourselves, this is time. We know ourselves internally in time but not spatially, when we think of ourselves, not of our body but of our self as conscious, we perceive no object, because space is an external intuition, this gives us the non-spatiality of the self. Perhaps counter-intuitively, Kant says that we can have no external sense of time whatsoever. Because it employs these *a priori* principles internal to consciousness, Kant calls his exposition of space and time metaphysical.

For us to understand things externally in space in different places the understanding of things as being spatial must already be the ground of any possible experience. Kant gives three examples that suggest the internality of spatial intuition: firstly, he says that we can imagine an empty space devoid of all objects, but that it is impossible that we could imagine no space at all. Secondly, he says that we intuit all of space as essentially united. Various objects can be in different spaces in the sense of being in different spatial locations, but all possible locations are within one, universal space. Thirdly, an aspect of our spatial intuition that differentiates it from the impressions of sensibility is that space is always understood as an infinity, whereas no object is ever so, we perceive all objects in their implicit limitation.

The status of the external intuition that is our in-built spatiality provides us, according to Kant, with an answer to the question we asked in the introduction of how synthetic *a priori* truths could be possible: if space is not something that belongs to things in themselves (noumena) and is not learned through experience, then it seems intuitive to believe that some of the things we know about it will be found to be true in experience. If we are going to project some image onto a screen, for example, and know which image we are going to project, we will thereby know what we will find projected, because we knew it beforehand. Kant says that any attempt to explain the presence of synthetic *a priori* truths that does not account for space as an intuition is doomed to failure.

Kant wards off the potentially creeping relativism at this point, saying that we designate all objects existing in space as external phenomena, thereby maintaining the objectivity of our perceptions. He is *saving the appearances*, to borrow a phrase[1]. He straddles the opposed viewpoints of empiricism and idealism by maintaining the reality of the spatial objectivity of objects, on the one hand, whilst affirming the *transcendental* status of space in its ideality. Not only is this the way things stand as regards our spatiality, but this external intuition of space is also the only intuition which grants us truth *a priori*. Space occupies a unique place within the system of transcendental idealism.

Kant now proceeds to a metaphysical exposition of time as inherent to the structure of consciousness. Just we found that we could subtract all properties of objects perceived through sensibility but could not do the same with the spatiality consciousness gives them, we also can not conceive of objects devoid of time, although we can imagine time without the existence of any objects. Kant states that we could conceive of things as existing neither at the same time, nor in any sequence unless time were already present *a priori* in consciousness. Time is the foundation of all of our intuitions. Just as space is given as a unity within which we differentiate a multiplicity of locations, we know time as a unified intuition within which we specify discreet moments. Likewise is time felt to be infinite and not limited in the way objects are. Time and space, under the conception laid down in the transcendental aesthetic, are not things of experience, they are *rules* by which experience as we know it becomes possible. This *a priori* sense of time is what allows us to understand succession. When we see an object in a space which was occupied by a different object, without our inner sense of time we could not conceive of the one object being there before the other, just as the co-occupancy of a single space by two different objects concurrently is a contradiction of the *a priori* space that is built in to our consciousness.

Time, having neither shape nor position because it is not a thing as such, is that sense by which we know our inner constitution. Our self-conception as not merely conscious beings but also as self-conscious. Time is the portal by which we gain access to our own being; but this is to leap ahead of ourselves. Space and time, as inherent features of consciousness, Kant says, the formal conditions of all outer and inner experience, respectively, and form the foundations of all mathematics.

Kant now addresses what he tells us is an objection to his ideas that is so common that he assumes it must occur naturally to his readers, it is regarding the reality of change. We are certain that we can observe things as they change, the shedding of the leaves from trees in autumn, the ever increasing number of grey hairs we see in the mirror. If time is an internal sense only, so the objector asks, how is it that we can observe these changes which are only conceivable as temporal developments? Let us recover what Kant has told us so far. Intuition is the primal ground of the possibility of empirical experience. Through sensibility we are given and understand sensations. Time and space are the forms of inner and outer sense. The phenomenon of the leaves being shed from trees is perceived through our structured consciousness, the phenomenon *is* that which appears to us. Trees have leaves at a certain time, and at another time they shed them and have them no longer. The trees, the leaves, are the objects of sensibility, and the having and then shedding is based in our inner sense of time. To try to think outside of this structure is to try to transcend ourselves as human beings, and to see into the things in themselves, *into their being as things not perceived*. But I see the change!, cries the objector, and indeed he does see the change, and the change is in time. But as time is a feature of our consciousness beyond which we can not go, the objective reality of the changes we observe is assured. What else is it that our objector wants, other than to go beyond himself and see the world as a non-human consciousness? The root of this type of objection is that Kant's transcendental aesthetic is so easily misunderstood as being the claim that time and space are not real. Something's being real and its being entirely separate from consciousness are not mutually exclusive. Our consciousness is real, unless we would like to maintain that an exhaustive ontology would not include consciousness. If we can loosen the grip of empiricist assumptions of what constitutes a thing's being real, then we can begin to think ourselves into Kantian philosophy.

2: TRANSCENDENTAL LOGIC

Kant begins the discussion of transcendental logic with an exposition of difference between it and the transcendental aesthetic. We perceive phenomena through the sensations that our sensibility receives, these are ordered and interpreted by the inner structures of consciousness that we call time and space. This is how perception works. The thoughts we have about these phenomena are our cognitions. There are, therefore, two general aspects of our conscious interaction with the world, sensibility and cognition. The aesthetic dealt with the laws of sensibility, now the laws of cognition will be our concern.

Kant distinguishes between two different conceptions of logic, the first being the system of formal rules that order the relations that hold between propositions, the second being the elucidation of the rules that hold sway in the region of thinking about the representations of sensibility. It is this latter type of logic from which the transcendental logic takes its name. Only that which applies to the a priori aspects of cognition come within the rubric of the transcendental logic, not the things which cognition thinks.

The transcendental logic is by far the longest part

of the Critique of Pure Reason and I have divided it into two chapters, one inquiring into what Kant termed the analytic and the other being dedicated to the dialectic. The former examines the formal structure of cognition that makes thinking about objects possible, the latter delves into the ways in which the understanding deludes itself through misapplication.

PART 1: ANALYTIC

Kant tells us that for an idea to belong within the analytic of transcendental logic it must satisfy certain conditions. It must be a pure *a priori* conception which has no empirical content whatever, remember that these are logical categories that enable us to think about the subject matter of our experience, not actual experiences themselves. It must also relate exclusively to the understanding of what we are given through sensibility, therefore it must not concern matters of sensibility nor of intuition. A further condition is that these must be elementary, singular notions, they can not be conglomerations of ideas that could be separated further into simpler categories. In addition to these conditions we must gather a complete register of the elements that constitute this transcendental logic which will account for all of the eventualities of thought, that is to say, we must lay out clearly the fundamental ground of our thinking.

Now it is important to highlight and prevent another possible misunderstanding of Kant's view here. It would be very easy to proceed by imagining that the way Kant envisages cognition working is somehow machine-like. That phenomena are processed by sensibility and ordered by cognition in a way similar to beef entering a grinder and reappears from the other end in the form of mince. Just like sensibility our cognition is something emergent, it is not to be likened to something that sits idle, waiting for input on which it then proceeds to work its magic and then *voila*, a thought is produced. What cognition and sensibility do, they do it spontaneously.

This feels all very abstract and it can be difficult to follow the path Kant is walking without concrete examples of what he means by his technical language. Put more simply, the sort of things that Kant understands as making up the form of cognition are generic ideas, such as divisibility, for example. Divisibility is a pure concept of cognition, we know what divisibility is without having any particular thing in mind that may or may not itself be divisible. So too do we understand what a body is without having an example in mind. If we say "this piece of a paper is a body, and it is divisible", the paper is of course the object of sensibility, whereas a body and divisibility are concepts by which the phenomena of our world are disclosed to us as comprehensible. Kant believes that these concepts fall into four groups, quantity, quality, relation, and modality. Each of these consists of three subcategories that Kant calls moments.

Quantity: Unity, Plurality, Totality.

Quality: Reality, Negation, Limitation.

Relation: Inherence, Causality, Community.

Modality: Possibility, Existence, Necessity.

Lists like these have the tendency to make my eyes gloss over by virtue of their extreme level of abstraction, however, Kant's idea makes a huge amount of sense when framed in real life usage. Let's take an example of something I currently see through my conservatory window: a garden statue. We will use this to illustrate the actual application of the moments of the categories.

First of all is the category of quantity. The first moment of quantity is unity. I see the statue, that it is alone in the sense that there is only one statue, it is a unity. The second moment is plurality. I can think of the statue as a unity (one statue) in a plurality (all the other such statues that were made). My individual statue is just one of many. Thirdly, this one statue, as it stands as a unity in a plurality, is part of the totality of all statues.

The second category is quality. In its first moment, reality, the statue is this unique statue that stands in my garden, it is my statue. It is weathered and discoloured, a small section of it has broken off. This is the reality of the statue. As this statue stands in its reality it is thereby a negation of every other reality that could be true of it but happens not to be, what philosophers call a counterfactual. That it is weathered is a negation of it being clean; that part of it is broken off negates its being whole and undamaged. This idea of every affirmation being an implicit and extensive negation was to have a deep influence on the thinking of a later philosopher, Hegel. These two moments taken together give us the last moment of quality, limitation. In being as it is and not another way, whilst negating all other possibilities other than its current state, the statue shows its limitation. It can not be undamaged *and* have a part of it broken off; it can not be weathered *and* clean.

The third of the categories is relation. Its first moment is inherence. The statue inheres as it is, as it stands in its place in my garden where I can now see it, and it continues to be there, inhering. In its second moment it is its causality. It stands on the earth, and in its standing it covers a small area of the ground beneath which its causality makes it possible for tiny creatures to have their dwelling. The inherence and causality of the statue not only shelters these beings from the harshness of the English weather, it discloses the earth as a haven for life, and in so doing it displays the third moment of relation which is community.

Finally we have modality. The moments of this category concern the being of the statue. Its initial moment is possibility. I could move the statue to a different place in the garden, that is one of its possibilities. Likewise I could paint it blue. It could not, however, transform into a horse or become an orange. Next is existence. The existence or non-existence of the statue is determined by certain conditions. It exists because I have not smashed it into a multitude of smaller pieces in which case it would cease to exist as a statue, for example, or if planet earth was no more. The final moment of modality is necessity. From the statue's possibility and its existence we arrive at the conditions which allow it to exist as it is. By necessity it must remain at a temperature at which it will not melt. Hopefully these examples will go some way towards making the categories more meaningful insofar as they are applicable in real terms.

Kant believes that, at this point, he has revealed the basis of the possibility of our experience, of what we call phenomena. The phenomena themselves are that which is known to us via the sensible and conceptual lens he has mapped out. This gives us the definition of the phenomenon as that which is disclosed by the type of consciousness we have investigated thus far. This serves as the juncture to Kant's next question: we have illustrated the categories which are inherent in consciousness without showing why, like the time and space of sensibility, they must be *a priori* rather than being derived from experience. After all, why is it that we could not somehow take causality on board after we have experienced the objects in the world, which could still be argued even if the conclusions of the transcendental aesthetic are granted. Kant calls this the transcendental deduction of the categories, it is one of the cornerstones of the *Critique of Pure Reason* and one of his most deeply insightful arguments.

I am looking out of my window into the garden. I hear the patter of light raindrops on my conservatory although the rain is as yet not substantial enough easily to see. I hear the sound of birds proclaiming that these are the last couple of hours of daylight. Kant sees in this experience a unity that we have not accounted for, that nobody before him had tried to account for. I hear the sound of light rain, but I do not see it; I hear the song of the birds without seeing them, and so on. We have seen hitherto that our consciousness is an integration of the two regions of sensibility and understanding. We know that sensibility is a receptor of what is given through sensation, therefore it would not make sense to attribute to it any kind of determining force. My conscious experience as I have described it is not a gathering together of raw data in the way the radical empiricists have tried to formulate it, it can not be, because my experience is not of disparate sensory inputs which I then cogitate into one seamless stream of consciousness, rather it is already given to my consciousness as a unity. Kant says that the spontaneous unity of experience, if it can not be interpreted as being given from outside, which evidently it can not, must instead be unified from within. The only explanation left open to us for the formation of the unity of experience are the features of consciousness laid out in the table of categories. The fundamental, inherent features of consciousness are what give us the unity of experience. To use a crude simile, we could say that this conscious unity is the glue that diverse things cohere. Thus, Kant believes he has deduced the categories transcendentally. He calls this the transcendental unity of apperception. Not only does this account for the unity of experience of phenomena external to us, but it relates also to the sense we have of ourselves as self-conscious beings. For not only are all the diverse and multifarious aspects of my experience unified in *a* conscious field, they are unified in the field of *my* consciousness. Even when I dream, I wake up knowing that it was *my own dream* that I had, not somebody else's, there is unity here too. That all of the experiences I have ever had, that taken as a whole I call my life, are contiguous though separated sometimes by many years, also speaks of the transcendental unity. In a very concrete sense this unity gives us the sense of ourselves. Our identity as individuals could be defined as the totality of what is held together in the transcendental unity of apperception. Kant says that this unity of apperception stands in relation to our understanding in the same relation as the aesthetic revealed the relation of space and time to sensation. He calls it an original power of combining the manifold and that it is the supreme principle of the understanding.

With the transcendental deduction complete, Kant recognises that an unanswered question has manifested. The moments of the categories, even if we accept that they are the ground of the possibility of the unity of apperception, are too vague to be in any directly useable sense applicable to the phenomena of experience. Causality under the categories, for example, tells us no more than that one thing stands in some relation to another. Unity is found not to be applicability. Kant says that there is another faculty which establishes the relation between that which is given to us through intuition and our thinking of them, he calls this the faculty of judgement. Judgement, in Kant's system, holds some kind of mediating position between experience and thought, being partly intellectual and partly sensible. I regard this aspect of his philosophy to be one of the most confusing areas of his entire *opus* and will for this reason pass over it very briskly. Suffice it for our concerns to say that judgement is necessary for us to form objective assessment of perceived reality. I state that the plant pot I see in the garden is round. I am in a passive relation to what I receive from the object as sensation, and the *a priori* categories operate spontaneously with sensibility to form representations. Judgement is the *active* element that we call thinking and deliberating. Remember that Kant believes that judgement performs a bridging function. The brave, or masochistic, reader who feels compelled to penetrate into the depths of this region of Kantian thought may choose to delve into scholarly literature beyond the scope of this introductory.

At this juncture, Kant turns to address what he calls problematic idealism, the types of idealism that assert that the existence of external objects is impossible to demonstrate. He mentions the philosophies of Descartes and Berkeley by name.
He takes aim at Descartes' ontology containing only one thing: himself. He accuses Berkeley of holding that objects exist only in the imagination. This is unfair to Berkeley, I feel, who is the philosopher most liable to being on the receiving end of straw-man arguments. Without digging too deep into Berkeleyan metaphysics, Kant claims that the way to the conclusion Berkeley will make to shore up his system of thinking is blocked on the grounds of him trying to speak of something imperceptible in the form of God. I believe Berkeley, with little adaptation, could turn an argument very much like this back onto Kant's discussion of phenomena and noumena, but I digress...

Kant's argument for the demonstration of the reality of external objects runs thusly: The transcendental unity of apperception granted us the continuity of the experience of the individual consciousness in time, internal intuition. For this continuity to be coherent, I must be aware of something outside of my self, transcendental unity can not be self-generated but must be dependent upon something permanent. Given that this must be outside of myself it follows that whatever it is it must exist in space, external intuition. The external intuition that is space applies to objects. Therefore objects are external to my self. Kant's establishes not only that there are things outside of me in the world, but also that I must know them, thus cutting off the idealist from making the move of asserting that objects may exist but that I can not know them to.

Kant's argument is the clearest statement he has made so far that his position is one of empirical realism. The objects of the world exist completely independently of our consciousness, were before us and will continue to be after us. It is only our *representations* to ourselves, of these objects, that are generated by consciousness.

Kant turns to the division of all things into phenomena and noumena, phenomena as things as we know them in our representations, and noumena as the things in themselves, as they exist outside of our perception and cognisance of them. The reader's knee-jerk response to this may be to object that things as they are noumenally are, by their very nature, cut off from us because they are not accessible to the type of consciousness we have described hitherto. Kant puts this concern away in a footnote to the section on the transcendental deduction of the categories, where he writes:

"...the categories in the *act of thought* are by no means limited by the conditions of our sensuous intuition, but have an unbounded sphere of action. It is only the cognition of the object of thought, the determining of the object, which requires intuition"[2].

Why does Kant introduce noumena at this stage, what, if anything, would be missing if he were to pass over the idea of noumena altogether? We have spoken hitherto about the things of the world as they appear to us, that they are represented to us by means of the internal and inherent structures of consciousness we have explored. An appearance is always the appearance of something that appears. I look in the mirror and I see my appearance, it is the appearance of me, of how I look. If all that we know of objects is how they appear to us, it would seem logically necessary to posit something of which these are appearances. This is the meaning of noumena. The numinous can never appear to us, of course, for that very appearing would make them phenomena. Kant says that it is perfectly non-contradictory, given what he has spelled out thus far regarding the nature of consciousness, that we should be capable of thinking of noumena. They are thinkable and reference-able by consciousness, it is only the definite knowledge of them that we are cut off from because all of our demonstrable knowledge is of appearances. Although this explains how noumena *can be thought*, it still does not answer the question of what explanatory work they actually perform and thereby the justification of their place within the system of transcendental idealism. The answer Kant gives to this turns out to be one of the points of greatest contention in his entire philosophical *opus*.. Why is it, given that our access to the world is limited to the appearances of objects, that we all perceive the same, or at least extremely similar, things when we make a collective observation? What gives us this transcendental unity of *group perception*, so to speak? Of course it is the noumena. We are not trapped inside our heads, lonely solipsists who inhabit impoverished, private worlds. Contrary to what Wittgenstein maintained, the world is not my world, it is my own personal view of an objectively real, independent world made up of the numinous. Only my perceptions are my own. Critics have objected that Kant is violating his own principles here, in regard to noumena, on the grounds that he is setting up a causal relation between the two. If phenomena are the appearances of noumena, and if we state that the appearances that we perceive are caused by the noumena, then we have attributed causality beyond its rightful place in the categories of our consciousness. I do not think that this criticism quite hits its mark though because if noumena occupy a place of *unknowability* in Kant's system, I do not see why he must be interpreted as establishing a *known* form of relation between noumena and phenomena. Kant himself says:"It is the consciousness of given representations to the different sources or faculties of cognition, by which alone their relation to each other can be rightly determined"[3], knowledge is determined by known relations, but he *denies* all possible knowledge of noumena. In other words, if the numinous itself is defined as *unknowable* then the way it interacts with consciousness itself could be equally unknowable. We may not know what nor how, but only that it is. If we are willing to grant unknowable things, I find it difficult to understand why we would have grounds to deny unknowable relations.

PART 2: DIALECTIC

Kant begins the discussion of the dialectic by telling us that is is a logic of appearances. Whereas the analytic gave us positive information about the structures of consciousness, the dialectic will take a more negative, critical turn as it works through examples of how we go wrong in trying to apply the categories to things which are not given to us through sensibility. In this section Kant begins to speak about something which has not received much mention so far, this is reason, which is surprising since we are in the *Critique of Pure Reason*. This tripartite structure is composed of sensibility, understanding, and reason. We can imagine this structure as one in which things are *given to us* in sensibility, then spontaneously *organised* by the understanding, after which they are *thought* by reason. Kant proceeds to the areas of thought in which he sees reason leading itself astray. Whilst not desiring to repeat myself overly much, I must say that it is absolutely imperative to remember that Kant is not dismissing the thinkability, conceivability, usefulness, desirableness, or otherwise of the ideas he treats of in the paralogisms. *He is refuting a definite set of arguments for them*. For example, it would be a mistake to come to the conclusion that Kant denies the existence of the self, rather he repudiates an argument. Kant is telling us that there are certain things in life which can not become the subject of scientific study, his thinking is an antidote to the scientism of our times, and we do him great injustice if we (mis)read him this way. That being said...

Kant begins his discourse on the errors into which reason leads itself with what he terms the paralogisms of pure reason. The first of these is the idea that the self, or soul, of a human being is a substance, an actual thing. We lead ourselves up this particular blind alley, according to Kant, because every one of our thoughts has, attached to it, an "I". I say that *I* see the table, *I* feel the cold breeze, and a myriad other statements, all have the form of attributing some property, or state, to something else, namely myself. Immediately the reader may ask "was the self not given to us by the transcendental unity of apperception?", no, it was not. What that unity gave us was the sense of the continuity of experience, it did not establish the objective facticity of the self as a substance. Reason is misguided when it allows itself to think that the self is a substance of which it can gain knowledge *a posteriori*, instead, the constancy of the "I" in the type of statements above points only to an *a priori* principle. That the self can be thought Kant is in no doubt, it is only knowledge of the self that he refutes, because as we have learned, all knowledge begins with experience. The next paralogism that

Kant turns his attention to is closely tied to the first, it is the belief that the self/soul is simple, and as such can be said to be immune from the decay which for all things physical is inevitable. This mistake is grounded in the inference of the substantiality of the self from the first paralogism, and that as differentiable from all material things it can be said to be simple and, as incorruptible, immortal. The third paralogism states essentially the very same thing as the first, and I confess that I do not understand why it requires restatement in different terms.

The fourth paralogism aims at the refutation of the argument that self/soul and world are non-identical. Descartes argued that because I am certain of my inner states and yet the state of things external to me may be uncertain, the self could not be of the same category of things as those we perceive outside of ourselves. Kant's attack on this self/world distinction idea is, perhaps, mislocated in this section of the *Critique*, and is rendered irrelevant by the argument from rigid designation made by the American logician Saul Kripke[4], which effectively drives a steamroller through arguments that the human mind is identical to any physical state of the brain.

After the somewhat repetitive arguments of the paralogisms, Kant moves on to what he calls the antinomies of pure reason. These are chains of reasoning regarding certain questions which generate two opposite, but equally valid conclusions. He gives us four antinomies, that relate to issues debated in his day:

Thesis 1: the world is limited in time and space, which is to say, the world has a beginning and an eventual end, and it is limited in size.
Antithesis 1: the world has no starting nor end point in time and exists eternally, so too does it extend in space without end, and is infinite.

Both of these ideas are false, according to Kant, because the world is an object of experience, a phenomenon, and neither of these lines of thinking rely on, nor relate to, any possible experience imaginable.

Thesis 2: the things of the world are simple, being made up of no constituent parts.
Antithesis 2: the things of the world are composite, being made up of simple, more fundamental parts.

From the point of view of the 21st century it is easy for us to declare that this is not an antinomy at all, but this would be unfair to Kant. If we replace his language about things with the language of the debates about fundamental structures of reality found in modern physics, such as string theory on one hand and quantum field theory on the other, then his insight can still be seen to frame within it an antinomy.

Thesis 3: there is free-will in the world.

Antithesis 3: everything is determined.

This antinomy contains a hotly debated topic not only in Kant's time, but one which continues to fascinate and frustrate today. Although this antinomy only gives voice to two sides, a third position is possible, that the two are compatible, and this is held by some, such as Peter Van Inwagen[5]. What is problematic about this antinomy is that the thesis may accurately describe things as they are in themselves, the noumena, whilst being false in regards to things as they appear to us, the phenomenal world. The antithesis has the problem reversed, we may well perceive things in the world to *seem* as though they are determined, but we may say nothing of the things in themselves.

Thesis 4: there exists some being by necessity.
Antithesis 4: all things are contingent.

This antinomy also hangs on the differentiation between phenomena and noumena, the thesis making a declaration about things as they may be in themselves, the antithesis extending appearances beyond phenomena.

Interestingly, Kant says that the rationalist philosophy develops along the lines of the theses he has given, whilst empiricism takes the line of the antitheses. The dialectic now moves on to consider some of the most well known arguments for the existence of God, and contains some of Kant's most widely celebrated ideas. Again, Kant was not an atheist, and was not arguing *against the existence of God*, rather, he was taking aim at some of the most highly regarded arguments for such.

The first of these arguments is that known as the ontological argument. This argument, originated by St. Anselm in the 11th century runs thusly: if we consider that God exists, this being would be perfect, infinite, ultimate, etc. Now if such a thing were to be non-existent, its perfection would be diminished, because a non-existent thing is lesser than an existing thing. It would, thereby, lack something, namely existence, and be rendered imperfect. Therefore God exists. Kant begins his critique of this argument by establishing that existence is not a real predicate. At this the reader may deeply sigh, crushed under the immense weight of boredom which all too often typifies the statements of the philosophers, just when we had built ourselves up for something earth-shattering. But let's give Kant a chance. Although dull types have lingered overly long on this aspect of the criticism of the ontological argument, it is far from the gist of it. The only thing Kant is trying to establish with this trivial observation is that the statement can not be analytic, can not be found to be true *a priori*. Remember that there are two types of proposition, the other being synthetic. Imagine I were to say that my garden gate exists; in order to ascertain the truth or falsity of the proposition we would have to go outside and find the gate.

We would find it to be true *a posteriori*, because the proposition is synthetic. Now we can see where Kant is going with this... The ontological argument sets itself up as an *analytic* truth, yet it makes a claim that can only be established *a posteriori*. In other words, the ontological argument is fatally flawed insofar as it is trying to be both analytic *and* synthetic, (which of course must not be confused with a synthetic *a priori* statement). Kant considers this to have put to bed the ontological argument. Personally, I am not convinced that existence is not a property that can be positively attributed to something. I find it difficult to conceive, for example, that spending time with my imaginary girlfriend would not be unsatisfying in some important way.

The next rational proof of the existence of God to be brought forth for criticism is that known as the cosmological argument. This argument follows a chain a reasoning that begins with the observation that things cause one another. The wind causes the tree to dance in its swaying, the varying temperatures in the atmosphere causes pressure that leads to the movement of the air that we call wind, the varying temperatures.... and so on. The cosmological arguments takes these chains of causality to their logical conclusion that ultimately there must be some *uncaused* beginning point which was the initiator of all subsequent causes. It is based on the belief that there can be no infinite regress.

This idea was present in the thinking of Aristotle. Kant's critical inroad into the cosmological argument is preceded by his acknowledgement that this way of thinking possesses the force of something which is intuitively valid. Not only that but he also concedes the correctness of the structure of the argument, his point of contention is that the conclusion of the argument leaps out of its own grounds and into the region of thought occupied by the ontological argument. Kant states that the thinking of the cosmological argument is freed only into the conclusion of an uncaused cause of all causes that is primary but not supreme, that is to say, the argument is only sequentially sound. In order for the argument to arrive at a supreme being it would have to form a valid reason as to why a originary cause must also be an Almighty God, as this is not analytically given.

Kant gives somewhat sympathetic treatment to the argument from design, in his terminology the physico-theological proof, which is the claim that the natural world itself offers clues that point to the necessity of the existence of a creator God to have made it. This argument is ultimately dismissed on the basis that what it gives us, at most, is an intimation of the existence of an architect, some force or being that guides the development of the world, but says nothing to the effect that there must be a creator who created the universe *ex nihilo*.

3: THE CANON OF PURE REASON

In the section entitled the Canon of Pure Reason Kant begins to open the path that will lead into the rest of transcendental idealism, this he identifies as the path of practical reason. The cardinal matters of interest for human beings are three, they pertain to the freedom of the will to choose and act, the immortality of the soul, and the existence of God. Pure reason can not help us in these directions.

Three questions frame the whole of philosophy:

1: what can I know?
2: what ought I to do?
3: what may I hope?

The first question has already been answered in what we have covered, we are armed with the knowledge of what knowledge is, and of what we can gain knowledge of. *The Critique of Pure Reason* is Kant's answer to the first question. The second question, that of what we ought to do, can not be treated by pure reason, ethics is wholly practical. What we can say about ethics in light of what we have learned so far seems to be very little. After all, we can not hope to find some ethical object from which we can form a representation, and thereby gain *knowledge* of ethics in the way we gain knowledge of trees, for example. Nor has Kant left the way open for us to lay claim to being under the command of an ordering and organising God whose guidance simply *is* our ethics. The fundamental criticism that Kant has made of empiricism is that it looks outside of itself for the key to explaining knowledge, whilst the answers lay within us all along, and only with the advent of the turning of our philosophical gaze inwards could we at last unlock the epistemological puzzle. So too in the subject of ethics, the answers we are pursuing have been sought outside of ourselves, in God, in nature, in social structures, etc., and our efforts have been frustrated because we were looking for something in a place where it can not be found. The foundation of ethics is nowhere in the world around us, it is within us, in our will.

A knee-jerk response to turning inwards in our search for the basis of morality might be to assume that this entails something like listening to our gut, following instincts, something entirely selfish. These types of actions are geared toward the end of making us happy, happy because our desires have been satisfied. Kant rejects this wholly personal version of ethics on the grounds of the observation that we can and do act in ways that are diametrically opposed to our own happiness. We do things because we feel duty bound to behave in such and such a way, even when it contradicts our desire. We stand up on a train to allow a pregnant woman to sit, we share our food with someone who has nothing, even though what remains will not satisfy our hunger, and so on. What we are acting on is a principle, a moral law, and it must be one which is *a priori* for obvious reasons. I think there is a possible objection here that is worth fleshing out. I stand on a train so that the pregnant lady can sit, I am acting against my desire for happiness in doing so. But what if these seemingly altruistic actions, whilst causing me discomfort in one respect, having to stand for the journey, can also make me happy in another way, such as winning the admiration of the other women on the train who observe and approve of my chivalrous conduct? Kant does not reject the reality of this, the point he is making is that we *can* choose to behave other than what our inclinations dictate, I may momentarily rise to allow the pregnant lady to sit, this would make me feel good, only then to change my mind and ignore her for the entire journey, making me feel ashamed of myself for being such a reprobate. Perhaps thinking of myself as a reprobate makes me feel happy, even so, I can always change my mind and decide to do otherwise. This being undeniably the case, Kant feels justified in asserting that ethical judgement is *rational* judgement. We can not, therefore, regard happiness seeking behaviour to count as moral behaviour, because moral judgement is principled, and as such it is defined by its beginnings, not by its ends. Happiness seeking is always teleological. In addition to this is the fact that we judge the moral status of our behaviour on the intention that drives it. Upon hearing the shout "STOP! THIEF!" I wrestle an entirely innocent man to the floor because I thought that he *was* the thief and my intention was to help. My behaviour was mistaken, embarrassing, hurtful, but not immoral. Ethical actions begin with intentions. The moral law also has the characteristic of being absolutely binding. If it is my moral obligation (it may not be) to allow the pregnant lady to sit then I am duty bound to do so, it is not conditional upon whether I am tired, or lazy. This is the sense in which the moral principle is rightly called the moral *law*.

Given these considerations, Kant believes that the only thing that can satisfy as a moral law is what he calls the categorical imperative. He defines it thusly: "I ought never to act except in such a way that I can also will that my maxim should become a universal law"[6]. This immediately leads to the conclusion that given we are able to choose how we will behave we must have free will, only a free will can be said to choose anything. For morality to exist, free will is necessitated.

Happiness can conflict with the moral law. Why should we choose one over the other? Free will is what gives us the ability to choose between different possible behaviours, but what ground have we from which to make such a decision? The supreme good will be when we can integrate the two directions of happiness seeking behaviour with the moral law itself so that in choosing to act morally we are thereby choosing the path of greatest happiness. But, Kant tells us, the mere coincidence of happiness and morality is not enough, we require a unification of the two, and this is discovered when we can make ourselves happy because we are *worthy* of happiness. Although happiness can not be the reason for moral behaviour, it is not precluded from being an outcome of it. This being the case, morality and happiness will be welded together into a glorious whole.

A problem is disclosed by this: if we behave in a morally good way, and yet, are not made to feel happy in so doing, then the supreme good is not achieved. Kant believes that if his reasoning so far has been solid, then he can conclude that the supreme good must be achievable beyond the scope of our earthly life. If we do not receive the reward of happiness that is our due, we must be right in hoping for it in the next world. From morality Kant derives his belief in life after death. If this is not grandiose enough a conclusion, he goes even further. For morality to be possible as such, justice must ultimately prevail. We see that it does not always prevail in this life, therefore there must be another life. The true judgement must take place in this next life. For the judgement in the next life to be final and fair, there must be a perfect judge who conducts the judgement, this judge would have to know everything that has ever happened in order to make a perfect judgement. This judge is God Almighty. Kant is not arguing for the existence of God as a phenomenal object in the world, this is after all the reason why he rejected the ontological and cosmological arguments, rather he thinks of God as noumenal. In this sense it could be rightly said that Kant is not arguing for the *existence* of God, if we understand the term existence to reference phenomena.

We have said enough of the Canon of Pure Reason to prepare the ground for us to proceed to the *Critique of Practical Reason* in its fullness.

4: PRACTICAL REASON

The first *Critique* set itself the task of determining how human consciousness and the world interact. It was an I & It affair. In this respect, Kant says, the *Critique of Practical reason* is markedly different from the first, for the relationship to be investigated is not one of self and other but of self to itself. The subject matter of the second *Critique* is the will and causality. Notice how radically this differs, as a foundation upon which an ethical theory is to be built, from those of other ethicists. Kant does not primarily look outside of himself to discover truths about ethics, but within. It is this inwardness that shows it to be a continuation of the earlier work.

Without hesitation Kant declares that there are principles in the field of ethics, they fall into either one of two groups: maxims and laws. A maxim is a principle that is understood to be applicable only to myself, whereas a law is a principle that is objective and as such applies to every human will in existence. A principle can only be considered to be a law if it can become a principle by which every will chooses to act. This principle, this law, when it motivates the ethical actor into ethical action, will itself be non-representational, it will not be the perception of an object of any kind. Now Kant sees this as extremely significant, because if the will is influenced, moved into action, by something other than sensibility, that means that it is being influenced in an *acausal* manner. Remember from the first *Critique* that causality applies only to phenomena. If the will can only be moved to action by the sensible, then we will have only ethical maxims, not ethical laws. Our personal principles, maxims, will be subject to our desires, which change in all manner of different ways, as we age, for example. Desire can not be the ground of a universal law, and all desires are of an equal standing. It will not do to claim that any desire is of a higher or lower rank or grade, the desire for sex is on an equal existential footing to the desire to help a homeless man by giving him money. Desire is desire. This elucidates the problem within the Epicurean conception of ethics, wherein the goal of all endeavour is the pursuit of pleasure. The various pleasures of diverse human beings can not be brought into agreement, and so can provide no universal validity. Reason, however, can not have a determinative effect on the will, because we must always have the freely chosen ability to to do otherwise, therefore these laws, grounded in reason, and moving the will to action, have the form of *imperatives*. An imperative takes the form of telling us what we *should* choose to do. Interestingly, Kant does not consider these universal practical laws to make any reference to the ends that ethical action might achieve. If we were to choose to tell another person the truth on the grounds that doing so would make them happier, this would not be a practical, ethical law, but it could be a personal maxim. Kant considers such iterations to be entirely empirical, and dismisses them as the possible basis for practical laws. This is because it would not be based within our own will, it would be a matter of us trying to effect something outside of ourselves. Whereas the proposition "one should always tell the truth", *could* be a practical law, insofar as it is a potential determination of the will that is not dependent on external contingencies. This precludes all forms of teleological ethics which, taken on the terms of transcendental philosophy, are no ethics at all.

"Act so that the maxim of thy will can always at the same time hold good as a principle of universal obligation"[7.] Kant does not suggest that we should, or even can, behave at all times according to such universal practical laws, we can do lots of things besides, but they will not be ethical actions. An objection here could be that it would be possible to formulate a universal law that applies to all others but does/can not serve as regulative for my own behaviour. This is not a possibility because if the maxim is found to be free of all empirical content then it is purely rational, in which case it must hold equally for all rational human beings, we are differentiated only by empirical things, and if we examine any potential candidate for a universal law that does not apply to ourselves, we will find it to contain empirical content, thereby excluding it from the category of universal laws.

Although Kant has already done away with the notion that ethics could be based in our feelings, he grants, or rather, accepts, that feeling does accompany our moral endeavours by necessity, they are feeling-toned. He calls this the feeling of respect for the moral law. We, as beings whose being is always beset with the impressions of the sensible world, can not rightly believe that we are ever rational in the sense that a being incapable of sensory influences could be. God, for example, is purely rational. If we were comprised of a purely rational will we would not experience the moral law as something that *limits* our behaviour. Instead, being as we are, the moral law more often than not takes the form of telling us what we are not allowed to do. The moral law has the effect upon us of overcoming our impulses, and so can seem to be a negative force, but this negativity is generated by the opposition of our sensual impulses *against* the moral law, not *by* it. Certainly, the respect we feel towards the moral law and its dictates is not the primary ground of, nor the original motivating factor in our conformance to it, and can not be lest we find ourselves back at the beginning with the feeling "ethics" of Epicureanism. It is the feeling that accompanies our moral actions, that makes us feel good in acting in an ethically sound way.

Kant completes his metaphysical deduction of

the categorical imperative with a discussion of autonomy. Autonomy is disclosed as the heart of all moral law because moral law must be freely self-given by a free will. This flips on its head the direction from which we approached the ground of possible ethical laws, which initial saw the human will as being subjected to practical laws which it found itself duty-bound to follow. Now we see that this subjection was chimerical, for it is solely from the substructure of the will's freedom that any such laws could be generated, and the subjection to the will to anything other than self-given law would be merely conditional. Kant's ethics turns out to be a freeing of the will into its ethical duty.

What has been uncovered in this exposition of the moral law is a *supersensible world*. Just as in the first *Critique* Kant showed us how the sensible world's existence was understandable under laws, now he displays the being under laws of a world accessible through the autonomy of pure practical reason.

Kant states baldly that although the *Critique of Pure Reason* served to delimit the region of all possible knowledge, as understood with all the caveats, at this stage of the *Critique of Practical Reason* we have gained a vantage point from which we can see into the beyond, past and through the limits initially proscribed, though they remain valid for what he called knowledge. Through this turning inward to the will, another world of thought has opened up for us, this is the noumenal world of which we can have no knowledge founded on sensibility. The autonomy of the will as revealed by the possibility of the moral law has granted to us our entry point into the noumenal world, the heart of being that all philosophers hitherto had erroneously sought through the operation of pure reason relating to the objects of the world.

We know causation to be a category of pure reason, not derived from sensation, and we know the will to be the causality of desire. So too do we know the will to be free will, and so we have unearthed the connection of causation in the realm of the noumenal. Because we can have no *theoretical knowledge* of the transcendent, Kant says that our application of reason must remain on the *terra firma* of what is practical. In this section Kant will analyse practical reason just as he did with pure reason, searching out the categories with which it operates.

The categories of practical reason to be addressed are the timeless ones regarding the nature of good and evil. Initially and for the most part we feel that the good is whatever causes us to feel pleasure, and evil is whatever causes us to feel pain. This conception, however intuitive it may be, leads quickly into difficulties, as it requires very little consideration to make ourselves aware of the difference between the good and the pleasant. Dental care is good, and yet far from pleasant in the estimation of most. A slight philosophical shift gives us the more nuanced and satisfying account of the good as that which engenders the pleasant, *vice versa* for the definition of evil. But this thinking of good and evil can not be decided *a priori* because pleasure and pain are matters of sensation rather than ratiocination. Plus, within this imagining of good and evil the two are reduced to mere means to an end and, this being the case, we find ourselves speaking no longer about good and evil, but usefulness. This thinking actually results in good and evil being left unthought. Further still, pleasant and unpleasant are terms that apply only to our personal condition or state, they are the affairs of sensation, and we have entered the realm of the numinous by virtue of the autonomy of the will, we must not forget that. If good and evil are to be profitably thought, they must be thought as things related in their being to the will. Good and evil can not be the names of things outside of ourselves that we relate to as representations; if there is an object of these terms it must be no other than the will of the man who acts. Here Kant posits the truth of the Stoic thought that neither good nor evil are to be found in the things that happen to us, neither in pain nor pleasure, but within the judgement of the man who experiences them to be so. Good and evil then, if they are to be conceived of as being other than judgements based on sensation, must be determined *a priori.* Kant says that this implies that something, i.e., the will, is good insofar as it conforms to the universal moral law, which is itself determined *a priori*, and bad when it is in contradistinction with that law. This is the only way in which we can avoid any contamination of practical reason by the empirical. It is also the only way for us to preserve the autonomy of the will, its freedom. Kant tells us that freedom is a type of causality, but one that does not hold between phenomena.

An interesting aspect of Kant's approach to ethics is that he can not be accused, as were the Stoic philosophers by Hegel, of being unable to establish a criterion by which to judge truth. This is due to the distinction he makes between the phenomenal and noumenal worlds. Kant not only does not establish a truth criterion, but to try to do so would be to slide outside of the transcendental system and back into the stagnant waters of traditional, *dogmatic* metaphysics. The truth that Hegel thought he was justified in demanding from the Stoics is the business of the first *Critique*, not of the second.

5: THE SUPERSENSIBLE WORLD

In the first *Critique* we found that after the elucidation of the categories of conscious thought paired with the pictures of the world given to us through our sensibility, that we were in a position to understand philosophical errors that preceded us and even to foresee those that may befall us in the future, just as the twin concepts of good and evil had to be clarified and distanced from other interpretations that did not fit into the transcendental system. Now we will investigate the way in which the critical philosophy can penetrate deeper into the noumenal world, from which life receives all of its value and meaning, to which Kant will later add beauty in his third *Critique*. This venture is fraught with danger, wrong turns and deluded efforts threaten to break into the metaphorical Noah's ark that is the system Kant has built up, and we must proceed slowly, carefully.

The practical wisdom this *Critique* has ultimately sought is the *summum bonum*, the greatest, highest good that man can aspire to. The ancients spoke of the love of wisdom and expected their philosophers to be not scholars but sages. Kant intimates to us that he would like something of that spirit to pertain in his system.

The moral law has been established as the supreme guiding principle of the rational will, but in its universality it loses the kind of concreteness that makes something relevant for everyday living, that secret, alchemical ingredient that transforms information into wisdom. It has no definite content, and is of interest to us purely due to its form, and is so by definition. The moral law is, must be, the driving force of the ethical life, as the *summum bonum* is its end, not end in any teleological sense, of course, but the place where our ark will come to rest after its sails have been filled with the winds of the moral law.

What precisely is to be understood when we speak of the *summum bonum*? Do we take it to mean the supreme good, insofar as it is found to be perfect and lacking in no way? Or do we understand it to be supreme in the sense that it is a whole which takes no place in anything greater? We understood virtue to be the *worthiness of being happy*, and this as the condition of all man's desiring as the place where all of our efforts ultimately wish to come to rest. But this aim is incomplete without acquiring happiness itself, after all, what is gained by the man who finds himself *worthy* of happiness and yet factually unhappy in his living? The *summum bonum* is, therefore, the conjunction of the worthiness to be happy, virtue, and the embodiment of that goal. Now Kant asks, are these two elements united by identity or by causality? The former being the relation that holds in the analytic truth, the latter that of the synthetic. He is asking: do we become happy because happiness is *present* as we render ourselves worthy of it? Or does happiness proceed from virtue, *given* to us as something that we qualify for as a result of it? Is the relationship causal or acausal? Kant considers the Greeks all to have held that the two are conjoined by identity, but that they took two juxtaposed approaches to the question, these being embodied in the rival philosophical positions of Epicureanism and Stoicism, respectively, with the Epicureans taking the stance that the fact that we find ourselves being happy itself is the grounding of the ethical life, and the Stoics holding that living virtuously thereby entails happiness. Neither concerned themselves with the possibility of a causal relation between virtue and happiness, indeed, they were so oblivious to this idea that they did not even take the time to dismiss it but passed over it in silence.

Kant rejects the possibility that these concepts can be found to be identical. Instead he diagnoses the very core of the historical disputations of the philosophers in this regard to revolve around their muddle-headed attempts to discover an analytical common ground for *heterogenous* ideas. He explicates this confusion by showing the intrinsic absurdity of the position of a man who is living in a virtuous fashion who only upon pondering the self-same nature of virtue and happiness *finds himself to be happy*, in fact, that he has been happy all the while without noticing it! Equally, the decidedly happy man who, one fine day, discovers that he is virtuous, *ipso facto*. This will not do. If this can not be unlocked analytically then the only way forward open to us is to treat it synthetically as a matter of causal relation, but this leads to a grave problem.

The difficulty that practical reason encounters in its trying to work out this solution Kant calls the antimony of practical reason. His account of it runs thusly: The summum bonum is practical, i.e., it is something to be realised by the will. Virtue and happiness necessarily conjoined. This conjunction must be either analytic or else it is synthetic. The concepts of virtue and happiness are heterogenous and, therefore, the relation between them can not be understood to be analytic. In that case it must be synthetic, if so there are two options: 1: we are driven to formulate maxims due to our desiring happiness.
2: Virtue is the efficient cause of happiness. The first is *absolutely* impossible, Kant says, because we have already found that all motives that are grounded in sensual ends do not even to enter into the moral realm, so nothing moral can be founded upon them. The second is also impossible because we can not coherently believe the will to establish a causative relation to the things of the world. If this is the case, then the moral law itself would seem to be false.

Kant's transcendental solution to the problem lies in the differentiation essentially between causing and being caused, although he does not ever state it this simply. When we treat the reality of the outside world not as it is in itself, but as the appearance we know it as, there is no contradiction in understanding ourselves, as noumenon, effecting the world in way that is causative and always in accord with the laws of nature, whilst *in ourselves* being the very noumenal in itself that dwells beyond the limitations of that arena. The laws of nature that we observe to hold amongst phenomena do not have their being in the world of the self. *I am a thing in itself*. The idea that virtue produces happiness is one that is false only if we conceive of the relation to be of the same kind that holds in the sensible world. This mistake remains open only to those who have not understood the transcendental aesthetic.

The relation of virtue to the actual enjoyment of a state of happiness is further clarified, Kant says, if we replace the term happiness with contentment. For the feeling of happiness is always fleeting and conditional upon the satisfaction of our desires, whilst dissatisfaction thereof results in unhappiness. In contentment, however, what we feel is a satisfaction of knowing that we are the captain of our own ship, so to speak, that we are not subject to the shifting winds of our inclinations. Virtue gives us the constancy of self-mastery. Kant draws near to Spinoza's concept of bliss in this depiction of the meaning of moral contentment.

Having secured the the understanding of the *summum bonum* Kant now turns to the question of whether or not this ideal can be achieved in life. In our pursuit of a perfect adherence to the moral law are we not, Sisyphus-like, rolling a stone uphill without hope of respite? Do our moral efforts extend us *infinitely* in the direction of saintliness? First of all, Kant considers the idea that a conception of pure practical reason could ever generate from out of itself an absurdity to be, itself, absurd. Reason can not give us an ideal unless it itself be reasonable, so unless we have made an error in our reasoning thus far, the ideal of the *summum bonum* must be attainable. This being said, no reasonable person could maintain the belief that we achieve the *summum bonum* except those few we rightly call saints. This seems to present us with a dilemma. How do we conceive of a *de facto* unreachable goal as being reasonable? Unreachable *and* reasonable? We can surely be forgiven if feel that there is a contradiction in these terms. Kant agrees that this would indeed imply a contradiction, but only if we consider the *summum bonum* as if it were an ideal confined to this bodily life on earth. Remarkably, he followed the dictates of reason so resolutely that he considered the possibility of reason being self-contradictory to be so utterly devastating to our lives that it grounded the belief in the immortality of the human soul. The alternatives are either that

Kant's philosophical project has made some unidentified error, of course he does not accept this, or that reason is not the guiding light of life, that it can lead us down blind alleys and wrong turns, in which case, what else do we have besides reason? Are we condemned to complete delusion *no matter what we do?* Before dismissing Kant's conclusion as being far-fetched or unjustified, it would be prudent to consider the implications for human existence if our faculty of reason were not trustworthy to guide us to correct conclusions. What would this mean for life, law, morals? We believe implicitly, without feeling the need to explain why, that whatever is reasonable is right, or that it is at the very least the best we can do. Kant has arrived at this conclusion because he has made himself subservient to reason, what are you, reading these words, subservient to when you disagree with his thinking? If the problem of morality can only be solved in eternity, which is Kant's contention, then immortality of the soul is not so much a matter of religious faith as one of practical disclosure.

If we are happy when things go according to the dictates of our desires, then complete happiness will be the condition of having *everything* go according to them. For this condition to pertain, therefore, we depend upon a state of harmony between our desires and the states of affairs of the things in the world. The difficulty we encounter in our quest for happiness is that we find these two elements to be in discord. For a will that exists as a thing in the world we can find no reason why the conditions that would lead to its maximal happiness should ever come to be. But in our investigation of the *summum bonum* we found that we had to postulate a connection between will and world as *necessary*. We came to this through an understanding of the self as noumenon. By the same token, Kant says that we can *postulate* the existence of a being that can bring about a state of affairs such that the degree of worthiness of happiness, which we have called virtue, is in exact proportion with the actual happiness of the virtuous. This being does not merely take the form of a rewarder of good deeds, but of a balance of happiness, better still, contentment and *moral character*. From this Kant concludes that such a being can not be rightly conceived as an impersonal first mover, uncaused cause of all causes, such as Aristotle thought, but it shows that this being is an *intelligent* one, which is to say, a rational being. This postulation of the existence of God is not ontological but moral. The moral law implies the *summum bonum*, the *summum bonum* must be achievable, to be achievable the soul must be immortal, for the conditions in which the *summum bonum* is achievable by an immortal soul, God must exist. It is important to add that Kant here is not adding to the list of the proofs for the existence of God, such as those he dismissed in the *Critique of Pure Reason*, rather, he is speaking about the *subjective* supposition that our actions only make sense within a given context, and that that context necessitates the immortality of the soul and the existence of God. It would be more correct, then, to say that Kant did not so much believe in the existence of God, but that he acted *as though* God existed and that we have an immortal soul; he is not claiming to have gained *knowledge* of these things in the theoretical sense of that word. This position has been repeated more recently by the psychologist and popular intellectual Jordan Peterson in his saying "I act as though God exists, and I'm terrified that He might"[8].

The explanation as to why the ancient Greeks could never satisfactorily solve the moral problem, that of the status and realisability of the *summum bonum*, is now brought into relief. The Stoics, even though they were correct in their postulation of virtue as being the originary pre-condition of the *summum bonum*, were still committed to the mistaken premise of the pre-eminence of the human will in its attainment. They had no conception of the will in its dependence upon anything outside of itself. Thusly, they placed the position that they were aiming to attain, that of the wise man, beyond the limits of their existence.

For Kant, the *summum bonum*, the postulation of freedom, and of the immortality of the soul, is the reason why we exist, it truly is the meaning of life. As he beautifully wrote: "Two things fill the mind with ever increasing admiration and awe, the oftener and the more steadily we reflect on them: *the starry heavens above and the moral law within.* I have not to search for them and conjecture them as though they were veiled in darkness or were in the transcendent region beyond my horizon; I see them before me and connect them directly with the consciousness of my existence"[9].

6: JUDGEMENT

Kant's first and second *Critiques* clarified the ground of knowledge and desire, what we know and what we want, respectively. Between reason, being how we purely think, and understanding, how we cognise, there stands judgement, as a middle term. Judgement is how we *evaluate*, and this evaluative faculty is the subject of Kant's third *Critique*. Having walked the critical path this far we intuit already the form of the investigation ahead. We are going to see if there are any *a priori* principles of the faculty of judgement, do our judgements grow from the soil of implicit workings of our consciousness, or do we learn them by *a posteriori* experience? We will examine the workings of judgement in an analytic, before searching out the ways in which this faculty goes astray, a dialectic. Whatever such principles this inquiry will unearth, they will not be *cognitive* principles, we do not know things of the world when we judge them, for if that were the case then they would be matters for the former *Critique of Pure Reason* to have examined. The *a priori* principle, or principles, are something that effect our feelings of pleasure or displeasure, but do not determine the ground of our desiring. Finally, this third *Critique* will not address the issue of en-culturing ourselves with a deeper appreciation of the beautiful, it will only ask what we do when we judge something on aesthetic grounds.

The *Analytic of the Beautiful* begins with the identification and explication of what Kant calls the four moments of taste, they are reminiscent of the moments we saw in the discussion of the categories in the first *Critique.* These are:

Moment of Quality.
Moment of Quantity.
Moment of the relation of ends.
Moment of the modality of the delight in the object.

When we form a judgement regarding the beauty of an object we use the power of our imagination, which Kant says, uncertainly, *may* act in conjunction with the understanding. The representation of the object has an effect upon the subject, our conscious mind, either in entailing the feeling of pleasure or of displeasure. These feelings are affectations of ourselves by the representations of things in the world. This means, by its very definition, that an aesthetic judgement *must* be a subjective one, and any hope of finding an objective "science" of aesthetic judgement is, on these terms, misguided.

The delight that we take in an object that we consider to be beautiful, that affects us pleasantly, is in no wise attributed to the real existence of the object in itself. Aesthetic judgement is the evaluation of a representation and, were we to discover that the object in question no longer exists, this would not effect a change in our evaluation of it. For example, if I consider a piece of woodland to be beautiful, that assessment is not altered when the woodland is destroyed to make way for a new road. Kant makes a distinction here between the beautiful and the good. The latter term he uses to refer to that judgement we make regarding the appropriateness or adequacy of a thing towards a given end. When we make a judgement as to whether or not the ladder in front of us is in good enough condition to bear our weight if we climb it, we must have already a concept of the end that the ladder is useful or useless as a means to. Aesthetic judgement falls under no such concept at all, as we can be affected by the beauty of something that we have never seen before and have no understanding of insofar as knowing its purpose. Indeed, beautiful things may well be the types of things that it would be senseless even to try to ascribe a purpose to. We appreciate the beauty of the natural world which for us serves no purpose. A decrepit old ladder upon which nobody of sound mind would climb could be considered to be beautiful. That we need know nothing in order to appreciate beauty is deeply intuitive and difficult to imagine arguing against, and what would Kant have made of the contemporary art that we have to "understand" in order to appreciate?

Kant now makes a distinction between three types of delight, a distinction which strikes me as somewhat counter-intuitive: He differentiates the agreeable from the beautiful, and both from the good. He says that the agreeable is what gratifies us, what is beautiful pleases us, and the good is what we esteem or approve of. He makes this distinction to contrast the difference between the feeling of delight we feel when we see a person who is a chef who we find beautiful, for example, and the delight we take in eating the food they cook. What I find confusing about this is that I am not sure what the difference would be between my delight in the agreeableness of the food and my delight in the food as good as a means to an end, the end that is the satiation of my hunger. Or is agreeableness a type of delight that we only feel in the satisfaction of our bodily needs and requirements? Perhaps these categories are fluid and something can be both good and agreeable? Kant says that "the judgement of taste is simply *contemplative*"[10], whereas the good is a judgement connected to the real existence of the object. If that is the case, then it would seem that the good is a combination of the contemplative judgement of taste and concern for the real existence of the object. I confess that this is unclear to me. Immediately after this Kant gives a definition of the beautiful that runs thus: "*Taste* is the faculty of estimating an object or a mode of representation by means of a delight or aversion *apart from any interest*. The object of such a delight is called beautiful"[11]. I feel that it is *factually incorrect*. Imagine two concrete situations, the first is a case in which a single person meets another who they find attractive and would like to become romantically involved with them; surely what they appreciate is a matter of taste, they recognise beauty. The second situation is of a married person who sees somebody who they also find attractive, and yet, due to the seriousness with which they regard their marital vows, they have no intentions at all beside the *uninterested* appreciation of beauty. According to Kant's definition, what is going on for the person in the first example is not a matter of taste, because it involves interest. I do not know how these two forms of appreciation, interested and uninterested, can be separated. I must admit that I do not understand what explanatory work the definition does.

Moving on to the second moment of taste: Quantity. In his unpacking of this moment of taste, Kant makes an extremely insightful statement regarding the nature of the appreciation of beauty and how this is assumed to relate to other people. He says that when I perceive beauty I must assume that I perceive something universal in which all others will find agreement. He is not saying, of course, that all are in agreement as to what is counted as beautiful, nor that they ever could be, but rather that within my appreciation of beauty I have no ground for understanding how another may not agree with me. I do not, can not, understand how another *fails to appreciate* the beauty of the thing before us. The beautiful is presented to us an object of universal delight, Kant says, and we can not see outside of our subjectivity.

Kant makes a distinction between the beautiful and the agreeable that helps (possibly) to shed some light on the difficulties of his earlier definition. He says that the agreeable is something that we appreciate as individuals only and will readily acknowledge that other people will be in disagreement with us. I can say that I find pears to be agreeable whilst accepting that others do not, for example. Kant says that because of this it would be incorrect to describe the taste of pears as something beautiful. The beautiful must be absolute, we can not see the possibility of it not being deemed to be so. Here we could make the objection that we could know through reasoning that other people are going to disagree with our assessment of the beautiful, but this would be a difference of *concepts*, and Kant is not discussing concepts here, rather the feeling of the beautiful. Beauty is not conceptual, nor is agreeableness, for then they would be the good. The second moment ends with a definition of beauty in light of it: "The beautiful is that which, apart from a concept, pleases universally"[12].

Third is the moment of the relation of the ends. In this section Kant discusses the possibility of rational purposes playing a part in aesthetic judgement. One aspect of aesthetic appreciation is that the beautiful feels as if it has a purpose. The beautiful yellow flowers that I now see in the garden seem to be beautiful for a reason, although we know beauty to be a subjective feeling of pleasure to which no purpose can be attached. Kant agrees that there is no real purpose to the beautiful, he is here interested only in its seeming so. We must nip in the bud any suspicion that a purpose of the beautiful may be ascribed on an empirical basis such as the power of the reproductive urge, and so on. This would be to make what philosophers call a category error.

Just because the appreciation of beauty is something subjective, insofar as it is determined by an object's being represented to a subject, does not mean that it is not related to the object. After all, I see a beautiful thing, I do not see a thing and separately see beauty. If this is the case then there must also be a temporal aspect to beauty, because phenomena are represented to us spatially and temporally. Were this not the case it would have serious epistemic anti-realist consequences that would cut to the heart of Kant's transcendental project.

The account of the third moment of taste ends with the assertion that there can be no objective criterion by means of which the beautiful can be evaluated. This is to say, that the idea of beauty must be kept separate from the idea of perfection, which is an aspect of the useful, or of the moral sense.

The fourth and final moment of taste is that of the modality of delight.

Whereas the agreeable is conceived of as actually causing the feeling of pleasure, the beautiful is necessarily connected with the feeling of pleasure, the pleasure I feel in the contemplation of the beautiful is inherent. Kant regards this as being possible only if we assume the givenness of a common sense of the aesthetically pleasing. Not common sense as we normally use that term in English, for Kant refers to *that* common sense as common understanding. Here he means a sense that is common to all. This may feel unconvincing, and many have found it to be so, after all, given a common sense of beauty would we not all be in agreement as to what qualified as beautiful? This is a mistake, Kant is not making *that* kind of claim, rather he is highlighting the possibility that we all share of being able to appreciate things we consider to be beautiful.

Kant distinguishes the beautiful from something closely related, but qualitatively different, this is the sublime, and he devotes an entire chapter to its discussion.

The beautiful and the sublime have in common that they are both pleasing by necessity, and that they rely upon neither a sensation (as in agreeableness) nor a concept (as in the good). Between the two, however, real differences pertain. Firstly, with regard to the beautiful, we always have in mind something that is limited, this is not so with the sublime. In fact, one of the key aspects of the sublime is that it engenders within us a sense of *limitlessness* and *totality*. The sublime has a fearful tint to it, it is what we call awe-inspiring. The sublime is more likely to be encountered in formless things, such as a sunset or a landscape, which is a situation rather than a static object. Due to this Kant says that the sublime is an indeterminate concept of reason, rather than one of understanding. Beauty is a judgement of quality, but the sublime is mostly a judgement of quality.

What is most archetypal in the sublime is the feeling that it elicits within us of its being something incomprehensible, something that exceeds the power of our consciousness to fully take hold of. The sublime makes us feel small, contextualised within an infinitely bigger picture of life and being. And unlike beauty, in which we behold the externality of the beautiful thing, the sense of the sublime tends to feel like an inwardness. Contemplation of the sublime often accompanies thoughts of the final things such as life, death, love, eternity. The sublime counts as being supremely important because in the imagination of the infinite we are lead, in a similar way that we were lead in the contemplation to the moral, into the supersensible realm of pure thinking. In the sublime we are confronted, hence its fearfulness, with that over which we can weald no power, something that defeats us. The sublime snatches us radically out of the everydayness of being and thrusts us into the spiritual reality that we call seeing the big picture. So too can the sublime effect us purely in thought. To demonstrate this imagine the fearful situation of being aboard a ship in the stormiest sea, were we really there we would feel utterly terrified and longing, praying, for dry land. But in imagining being aboard such a one we can feel a certain pleasure, a thrilling feeling. The sublime has the power to command our feelings even when we are not in direct contact with it.

The dialectic of judgement, Kant says, will differ from the dialectics of the former two *Critiques* in that it will not be a dialectic of aesthetic taste itself, for no definite deduction can be given for such judgements, rather it will be a dialectic of the critique of taste. The antinomy is presented in these two statements: 1, that the judgement of taste is not based upon concepts because if it were then we could reasonably hope to resolve differences of aesthetic judgement definitely, and 2, that aesthetic judgement is based upon concepts, and that if it was not then it would leave us no terms on which to disagree about our relative judgements, because they would lack any common ground. Kant's handling of this is deeply insightful. He says that the pleasure we feel when we contemplate the beautiful is the *free play* of the faculties of imagination and understanding. This freedom would not hold if it were ruled by a determinate empirical concept. However, the opposite of rule following is not freedom but chaos. That beauty is pleasurable to behold is testimony to the fact that the free play of the faculties is under a rule, though *indeterminate*. This is mirrored in the freedom of the will, which is free and under the moral law. Kant is assuming, fairly enough, that our individual human consciousnesses are similar enough as to be comparable, that we all take pleasure in the beautiful gives us sufficient reason to believe that the free play of the imagination and understanding in all people moves in the same way.

Kant's solution to the antinomy hinges on his distinction between phenomena and noumena, this reveals how and why the third *Critique* fits into the system as a whole. The free play of the imagination and understanding in the appreciation of the beautiful is possible only on the grounds that the self, as noumenal, is not subject to the determinate laws that govern the world of phenomena. Aesthetic judgement turns out to be under the rule of something wholly internal, transcendental. Here, as in the disclosure of the moral law, we gain intellectual access to the supersensible realm. The sheer quantity of forms of beauty within the natural world, Kant believes, give us further reason (literally) to think that the phenomenal world is grounded in the noumenal, and that only the account of the world given in transcendental idealism can satisfactorily appropriate these facts. This is why beauty and morality are closely connected in Kant's thinking.

CRITIQUE

Kant's thinking has been immensely influential, directly illuminating the way for Fichte, Schelling, Hegel, and Schopenhauer, even as they disagreed with him. His idea that the human being should be placed at centre stage methodologically, was a startling novelty in his time and intimates one of the essential elements of modernity: individualism. The psychologist Carl Jung once described himself as being steeped in the philosophy of Immanuel Kant, and it is difficult not to see the influence of the phenomenal/noumenal divide on Jung's conception of the archetypes of the collective unconscious as being things only known in their appearances whilst remaining unknowable by direct perception.

One of the most fundamental features of the Kantian project feels problematic to me, that is the belief in reason's ability to analyse itself. I philosophise about sensation, for example, from a position outside of sensation, by necessity, because sensation can not look at itself. *That* observation is then observed from a position *outside* of this second viewpoint. The problem is that the critical position, regardless of how far it gets removed from its beginnings, must end up examining its own ground if it is to avoid an infinite regress. At whatever point we decide to cease from our investigation, and that point will always be arbitrary, we will be left with the dilemma of doubting whether the faculty we conceded to be final actually has the ability to examine *itself*, like trying to look at our glasses through those same glasses. Any fault in the lens will be seen whenever we look through it. We must, it seems, arrive at some place from which reflective thinking is no longer possible, pure phenomenal consciousness perhaps, at which point, to paraphrase the Heidegger scholar Lee Braver, we are on the groundless grounds of our thinking. What is the ground upon which Kant's thinking is *given?* A somewhat similar situation would transpire amongst mathematicians in the early years of the 20th century as they embarked upon the project of establishing logical foundations for mathematics.

As regards Kant's thinking through the issues of the immortality of the soul and the existence of God, I for one can not help thinking, even if his reasoning is technically sound, that he is thinking things into existence. That is to say, something's making sense to our finite, rational minds does not, can not, posit the said things into existence. The world is obliged to make sense to us, it it were, perhaps Kant's thinking along these lines would hold. It ultimately comes down to whether or not we accept the principle of sufficient reason.

Contrarily, the feeling function of the *Critique of*

Judgement provides something that has been lacking from the history of Western philosophy. Great prejudice has typified the preference of thinking as some abstract, mechanistic, way of thinking over and above the feeling-toned reality of our everyday experience. This bias is what has lead, in our own time, to the technological aim of re-creating consciousness in a computer. Only if consciousness is computational, rather than feeling based, is this a conceivable goal. That consciousness is irreducibly connected to feeling seems to me to be so intuitively assured as to need no justification. Perhaps this is why Kant considered his third *Critique* to be of such fundamental import, and also why the Western intellectual world has so resolutely ignored it; philosophy has not paid sufficient attention to emotional life, in fact it has shunned it. The importance of the third *Critique* within the overall system of Kant's thought may lie in its bringing philosophy concretely into the everyday world in which we dwell.

REFERENCES:

1: Barfield, O. *Saving the Appearances: A Study in Idolatry.* Barfield Press. 2011.

2: Kant, I., *The Critique of Pure Reason.* Meiklejohn, J.M.D. (translator). University of Chicago. 1952.

3: *ibid.* page 99.

4: Kripke, S.A., *Naming and Necessity.* Harvard University Press, Blackwell. 1980.

5: van Inwagen, P., *An Essay on Free Will.* 1983.

6: Kant, I., *Groundwork for the Metaphysics of Morals.* Oxford. 2019.

7: Kant, I., *The Critique of Practical Reason.* Meiklejohn, J.M.D. (translator). University of Chicago. 1952

8: Kaczor, C., Petrusek, M., *Jordan Peterson, God, and Christianity: The Search for a Meaningful Life.* Word on Fire Institute. 2021.

9: Kant, I., *The Critique of Practical Reason.* Meiklejohn, J.M.D. (translator). University of Chicago. 1952

10: Kant, I., *The Critique of Judgement.* Meiklejohn, J.M.D. (translator). University of Chicago. 1952

11: *ibid.*

12: *ibid.*

Printed in Great Britain
by Amazon